WE WON'T BE SILENCED

AUDREY LEE O'DONNELL

We Won't Be Silenced

Copyright © 2024 by Audrey Lee O'Donnell.

All rights reserved. No part of this publication may be reproduced, distributed, or transmitted in any form or by any means, including photocopying, recording, or other electronic or mechanical methods, without the written consent of the publisher. The only exceptions are for brief quotations included in critical reviews and other noncommercial uses permitted by copyright law.

MILTON & HUGO L.L.C.
4407 Park Ave., Suite 5
Union City, NJ 07087, USA

Website: *www.miltonandhugo.com*
Hotline: *1- 888-778-0033*
Email: *info@miltonandhugo.com*

Ordering Information:
Quantity sales. Special discounts are granted to corporations, associations, and other organizations. For more information on these discounts, please reach out to the publisher using the contact information provided above.

Library of Congress Control Number:		2024923494
ISBN-13:	979-8-89285-378-1	[Paperback Edition]
	979-8-89285-379-8	[Hardback Edition]
	979-8-89285-380-4	[Digital Edition]

Rev. date: 11/07/2024

Contents

Preface vii
Acknowledgments ix
Chapter 1   Sexual Health Education 1
Chapter 2   Menstruation 6
Chapter 3   Pleasure 16
Chapter 4   Abortion 25
Chapter 5   Birth Work 30
Chapter 6   Reproductive Advocacy 35
Chapter 7   Teen Pregnancy 44
Chapter 8   Toxic Masculinity 49
Chapter 9   Body Image 55
Chapter 10   LGBTQIA+ Experiences 70
Chapter 11   Birth Control 79
Chapter 12   Domestic Violence and Sexual Assault 85
Chapter 13   Sexually Transmitted Infections 91
About the Author 95

Preface

When I was seven years old, my sister Deirdre was pursuing gender studies and took me with her to study often. I was all the more curious about the work she was doing, and I knew that one day, I wanted to be as empowered as her. When my sister performed in *The Vagina Monologues*, I grew interested in the world of acting and making a difference. Once the performance was over, her friends commented on how young I was at such a seemingly "mature performance" and how I am "yet to become a resilient young woman." My sister hugged me and said that I already was one.

As a sophomore in high school, I searched for an internship within the field of performing arts.

I contacted my sister inquiring about internships, and she mentioned her old college where I could conduct potential HIV/AIDS prevention work. At first, I said, "Absolutely not. I'm not interested." I was caught up in the stigmatizations around sexually transmitted infections (STIs), which made me apprehensive toward doing such work.

Post-introductory meeting with my advisor and future mentor at the Diversity, Equity, and Inclusion (DEI) Center, my advisor and I grew very excited. I felt as though she believed in me; she knew that I was yet to do big things because of this internship. Thank you, D.

My first few months in the DEI and Women's Center consisted of learning all about social justice. My mentor inspired me that I could use my power as a young person for good, that I could make a change. Yet I was lost. What was it that I wanted to do?

In December of 2017, the college held a panel where people living with HIV/AIDS shared their stories. I became so interested in their stories that I wanted to do more surrounding this topic. Immediately after listening to the panel, I went home and made a timeline for a project where I would teach about HIV/AIDs in the hopes of lessening the stigmas surrounding it. As a result of my teachings and research, I learned that young people need (*need, need, need!*) sexual health education. Was my emphasis on need big enough?

Acknowledgments

Thank you to each mentor, advisor, friend, activist, interviewee, and supporter who made these stories come to life. We are working to reduce the stigma one story at a time.

Chapter

1

Sexual Health Education

What would the world look like without stigma around sexual health education?

sexy

healthy

safe

informed

feminist

communicative

What was your experience like with sexual health education in schools?

"I didn't learn very much. I was left with a lot of questions, leaving me turning to the internet which has lots of scary sh——t."

"I think my peers and I had pretty good sexual education in terms of the content and topics they taught us about. However, I think there could've been a lot more classes given to us. Instead of it being just one class once in a blue moon, I wish we would've been given more classes often throughout the years."

"Never had any! So now I'm a sex educator. :)"

"In comparison to and in context of the state of US sex education in the mid to late 2000s, it was pretty good. I learned anatomically how sex happens, body parts, and how babies are made in third grade in Catholic school (purely from the 'sex is for making babies amongst married men and women' perspective in 2002). In seventh grade, I remember being taught a very uncomfortable and awkward health class from the white cis-male gym teacher/wrestling coach (we were forced to watch a very clinical and gruesome depiction of a woman giving birth that was meant to look awful enough to discourage us from having sex with each other). In ninth grade, I had a queer woman teach us all about every kind of birth control and sex (anal, oral, penetrative) and STIs, and lots of mention of sex for pleasure. We got a great overall introduction to the basics by a crucial age (*all* ninth graders were required to take this class), which is *way better* than what a lot of people learned both then and now. However, there was barely any mention of variances on queer sexualities, nothing on relationships or structure (healthy or otherwise), *nothing* on consent or body image. Again, it was much better than most but *not* extensive enough at all to make informed, healthy sexual choices for the right, empowering reasons."

"Since the third grade, I have been 'taught' about health. Those outdated videos where they show us the body changing and how girls' periods would start soon and how the boys' voices would drop. They would separate the boys from the girls when talking about health. That's where stigma is created among children. Boys wouldn't know about the female body, and whenever conversations like periods, tampons, or pads would start, they'd have disgusted/grossed-out reactions. Separating them at an early age allows boys to be oblivious to what is natural in human bodies."

"I was part of this wonderful health information program in high school. We (juniors and seniors) would be trained to teach health education to our freshmen! We had over ten sessions over the course of the school year. It honestly taught me so much about life and people and even so much about myself, and being able to bring that and teach it to other people made it so, so, so much more special for me! Be smart! Be healthy! Be HIP!"

"It would be so freeing to not be worried about others' opinions of my sex life. Especially for girls. It's like when a guy loses his virginity, it's celebrated, but when a girl does, it's somehow a loss of her innocence. A lot of the stigma is what creates my anxiety surrounding sex."

Chapter

2

Menstruation

During my first week of freshman year, I got my period. I was fourteen and felt behind compared to my peers. While coping with injections for my growth hormone deficiency, I was led to believe by my friends' parents that I was a so-called *late bloomer* which came with the incessant comments on a future growth spurt (which never happened by the way. I'm *deficient*!)

When I got my period, I was sick with a sinus infection and thought I was dying. Yes, dying. I screamed for my mom to come into the bathroom as there was blood all over my pajama bottoms after waking up. While I experienced an anxiety attack, my mom was jumping up and down clapping for me saying you *finally got your period!* I could breathe again, but I felt a mix of emotions. Not only was I struggling to breathe between the congestion and anxiety attack, but I finally got my period! My tears of fear turned into tears of joy and I finally felt like my body was working for me.

When I felt the wave of cramps, I told myself I could have waited longer, maybe even forever. I had never felt pain like that before and nobody could have prepared me for it. Through the next year, I dealt with unbearable sharp pains when I sat down and could not bend over. It was so severe, I was throwing up and had to see a doctor. They told me I had PCOS. What the f——-k was I supposed to know about PCOS. My pediatrician explained that it is Polycystic Ovarian Syndrome. I shook my head, still in utter confusion. *What?* She explained that I had a cyst on my ovaries and that it would pop on its own with rest and a warm compress. *What's the worst that can happen?* I asked. I was told that my cyst could develop into a chocolate cyst, and I would need my ovaries removed. I was only fifteen.

My period kept me out of school, jobs and internships quite often. Due to stigma, I spent a lot of time thinking that it was something that I could adjust to. Impossible! It was not until I turned 21 and began using the birth control pill. After being instructed to take the pill continuously, I stopped getting my period and the cysts disappeared. I have not had one in two years! For a long time, I did not have health insurance. I had to pay out of pocket for my birth control and if I had little to no funds, I had to find a cost-effective or free way to access pads and tampons. Without access to birth control, I would be incredibly sick often and at risk of needing an emergency hysterectomy.

As a part of the *We Won't Be Silenced* mission, we collected thousands of menstrual products by donation from different countries, celebrities and menstrual drives which were dispersed to high schools, domestic violence and homeless shelters.

AUDREY LEE O'DONNELL

What would the world look like without stigma around menstruation?

honest
unrestrained
free fair happy
progressive
equal peaceful

What do you wish you had known about periods before menstruating?

"That I should have been exploring my own body long before and becoming comfortable with it."

"I wish that I knew more about menstrual cups!"

"We shouldn't feel shame around it."

"That it's totally normal, and no, you're not dying."

"There is a difference between normal period-related discomfort and pain due to menstrual disorders. You are not weak or complaining if you can't sit or stand up due to menstrual pain. Menstruation is extremely varied and unique to each person. And our healthcare system has never focused on exploring those complex variance of experiences, so what we know is just the tip of the iceberg."

What was your first experience menstruating like?

"Mortifying. It was the day before I started sixth grade, and I was staying the weekend at my dad's house. I had the choice of asking my stepmother for help, and I wasn't very close with her, or going to my dad, who had never expressed any interest in talking to me about these issues. I went to my dad and burst into tears. He didn't know how to talk about it, so he clammed up and called my mom. Had he been more comfortable about this, had he prepared for his daughters, or had he not been immediately embarrassed and repulsed, I feel like I would have had a very different experience."

"My sister had her period before me, so I was sort of educated, along with health class at school. So I was in eighth grade when I got it. It wasn't shocking to me because I've seen my sister having cramps and leaking blood through clothes. I was at home, and I had my mom, so my mom helped me. I was happy at the same time, 'cause everyone seemed like they already got their periods, and I felt sad that I hadn't got mine. But when I did get it, I felt like I was finally one of them."

"I remember when I first got my period. I was about twelve, and my mom never talked to me about it. The toilet water was red, and I was so nervous I didn't tell anyone. I grabbed my iPod Touch and googled it (because where else can you find the answers to all your health questions!). I only found articles about cancer—nothing about menstruation. The lack of information out there led me to believe I was in serious trouble, although I never said anything. In addition, that goes to show the stigma around menstruation. I'm eighteen, and my mother to this day has never talked to me about it. She bought me pads once and never said anything. I don't even know how to use a tampon."

"My first period was extremely painful and scary. I was fifteen and also the last person in my friend group and family to get my period. I figured out I got my period at my dad's house when it was just the two of us. I cried on the phone to my sister, who was away at college, and as loving as she usually is, she was a busy nineteen-year-old and told me, 'Everyone goes through this. It's not that big of a deal.' My dad offered to get me 'whatever products you need,' and I was mortified while accepting his help. I didn't know at the time that I was experiencing cramps for the first three days of my period or that this is what would happen during every period I would have since. The next day at school, my cramps were so painful that I was having a hard time sitting in class and standing up during school. When I sat in class bawling over my desk, my teacher told me to call my mom. My mom told me, 'I'll let you go home this time, but you're going to have to learn how to deal with this.' While that has proven to be an unfortunately accurate statement, at that moment I thought I was just complaining and this is what happens to every person menstruating. I didn't know until ten years later that I have endometriosis."

If you have experienced extreme period pain, what was it like seeking help?

"I have extreme period pain often to the point where I vomit because my cramps are so intense. No one else in my family experiences this. My mom, my sister, my aunts, and my grandma all have or had light, easy periods. Because of this, no one believes me when I say how bad the pain can get. I must be faking it. I must be overreacting. The pain isn't as bad as I say it is. Their personal experiences have completely outweighed my own. I have gone to my mother numerous times about going to a doctor, getting birth control, looking for some sort of diagnosis, but no one has taken me seriously. Since the pain started three years ago, every single month, for at least a day, I have been sick to my stomach, often crying in pain, but no one will listen. I wish I had known longer ago that I know myself better than anyone else does. Only two days ago, I went behind my mother's back, who doesn't want me on birth control because it is 'unnatural,' and scheduled myself an appointment to discuss my pain at a reproductive health center. I hope this helps."

"It has been exhausting and to very little avail. I started seeking help for my period pain when I was nineteen and my pain had become debilitating every month and I had extremely irregular periods, never knowing when my symptoms would hit. I have met with somewhere between five and ten doctors, and pretty much everyone either didn't believe me, told me painful cramps are normal and to take six ibuprofen while symptoms last, or to take birth control indefinitely. Lots of dismissal or 'This is what I know, and this is all I can do. Take it or leave it." To get anyone to take my pain seriously enough to consider testing/exploring for period disorders took years, and it was actually a nurse and doctor at a reproductive health center who were the first to take me seriously and suggest that I might have PCOS or endo. My most recent doctor said she believes that I have endometriosis (but to confirm, I can do a pelvic sonogram or undergo an invasive surgery, both of which I cannot afford to do under my insurance plan) and recommends taking birth control to shut off my menstrual cycle and skip my period entirely so I never experience one. It's nice to have someone believe me and want to treat me, but I also hate that I both can't afford to continue with my next healthcare options and that the only option for a person in my situation is to entirely shut off and alter my reproductive system. I feel very connected to my moon cycle and would love for there to be more options to people who menstruate than just shutting off a natural cycle, particularly in a time where the long-term effects of birth control aren't always known because they are relatively new and research is underfunded and developed."

"My daughter is eleven, and although she hasn't gotten her period yet, I feel like it's about to happen. And when it does, then what? Will she be embarrassed? Too ashamed to talk about it to me, her father? Or proud that she has reached a biological milestone, like the way she felt when my finger held the tape measure at the top of her head at the 4'9" mark, proving that she could now ride in the front seat? I grew up with a brother, so I've never been in proximity to a girl experiencing her first menstruation, or the parental responses to that period. Do I let Mom handle it? Do I wait until she wants to mention it, if ever? **Or does *not* asking or talking about it send its own kind of stigmatizing message?** I've never heard dads I know talk about this challenge. Are all of our heads in the sand? I want to keep my head on what's best for my daughter."

"I think the misinformation around it, especially by people who don't have periods, can often be the reason why girls can feel ashamed. I remember in middle school, whenever I or another girl would get upset, this guy would taunt us by saying, 'Oh, are you on your period?' and that felt really discouraging and invalidated our feelings."

"I obviously had my own struggles with my period, but I learned so much more about period stigma and period poverty when I began working at a nonprofit for the menstrual movement in 2019. I hadn't even considered the lack of access aspect and learned so much about how interlocked period stigma and poverty are."

"Period pain is often so misunderstood, even by women. It's something we must suppress or hide because it's shameful and dirty. It happens every month; I can get used to it. You're a woman; you must be exaggerating. No one wants to hear about it; stop complaining. Every woman has experienced it; it's just a part of life. It's pain. It's painful. It's debilitating at times. It should be treated like any other pain. It should be taken seriously. It should not be dismissed, especially by other women."

"I think women or teens shouldn't be scared to talk about menstruation 'cause it's something that happens to all females. And not everyone gets their first period around the same time, so I think people should be aware that everyone is different."

Chapter

3

Pleasure

There is no doubt that a significantly large taboo around sexual pleasure exists, and it is not something that affects just one gender—it affects all identities. Oftentimes, talking about pleasure may feel uncomfortable at first. But why does it have to feel that way? When we see posts about it on social media while in public, we quickly scroll past it, or we even experience discomfort and sink back in our chairs. It has become common to feel shame surrounding pleasure because of our society, which does not promote positive reinforcements for our sexualities. Some nonjudgmental comprehensive sex-ed programs do a fair job in teaching about pleasure, yet other times it is left out. For something that is healthy and common, why should it be stigmatized as much as it is? In order to deflect the source of shame, we must be conscious of where the stigma is rooted from.

I volunteered at a health fair when I was seventeen years old. I was visiting tables, and once I saw a table about sex toys and pleasure, I was not sure of what to say to the people who were working. Funny how a seventeen-year-old sex educator reacted that way, right? Well, it was because I still experienced the effects of stigmas around pleasure. I asked myself, *Why did I react in such a way?* and realized that it was because I felt "too young." Younger people are conditioned to believe that they are "too young" for "adult conversations" about things like pleasure and sex. I can't even count how many people above the age of forty told me that I was "way underage" to do the sex-education work that I conduct. This only leads us to be apprehensive toward being open to adults as well, asking questions and simply being curious.

Several years ago, I was at lunch with my friends, and somebody began to open up about pleasure. An individual at the table quickly interrupted and said, "That's disgusting." I made a comment about how pleasure *is* stigmatized and how we are taught that we shouldn't speak of it. At first, they appeared confused and then had this moment where it looked like a switch went off. They responded with "Oh . . . I've never thought about it that way. Thank you!" They then turned to the person who had been talking about pleasure and said, "I'm sorry. Please continue." It's these moments and learning experiences that help us grow. While it is important to adapt to these changes, it's vital to make sure that we don't call people *out* when they're confused or are lacking information but to calmly call them *in* and redirect or help them instead.

AUDREY LEE O'DONNELL

What would the world look like without stigma surrounding pleasure?

happier
healthier
less stressful
enjoyable
accepting

WE WON'T BE SILENCED

What positive word(s) do you associate with pleasure?

control

natural

fun

safety

vulnerability

freedom

excitement

feeling good

hot

sexy

joyous

empowering

life-altering

freeing

feminist

In a just world, what would pleasure look like for everyone?

"Frequent, empowering, a concept that every person learned about early and as vital to all partners involved."

"Pleasure would and should look like the ability to enjoy what one finds pleasurable without fear or judgment."

"Everyone would feel like they deserve to have pleasure, and it would be okay for them to seek it out."

How was pleasure talked about in a shameful or positive way in your family, friend groups, etc.?

"Pleasure was spoken about in a positive and feminist way from my mom and her side of the family. It was clear that sex could and should be pleasurable, but there wasn't any discussion about how to explore that or communicate it to make it happen for all parties involved. It was clear from my mom's community that women's pleasure during sex is important, but no logistics or details. There was no discussion about pleasure at all from my father or his side of the family"

"Family always said it was normal and were very open—this led to me being more open-minded."

"Pleasure was looked down upon in my family. My parents told me not to have sex and taught me that it isn't for enjoyment."

"I feel like my family is pretty conservative in that area, and then growing up going to church and being told that it was a sin makes me feel like a bad person."

What was a positive or negative experience that you've had around pleasure?

"When I first started exploring my sexuality, as a person with a vagina exploring sex with a person with a penis, I thought sex was something that was going to happen *to* me. I thought the first time (or first several times) were just going to be painful and be over when they finished, and eventually it would feel good and be for my pleasure. The first time I tried, I was seventeen and thought I was getting too old to be a virgin and just wanted to get the first time(s) 'over with,' but I didn't end up going through with it. The next time, I was doing it for the same reasons at eighteen and didn't trust the person I was with. It was much more painful than I thought and stopped it very quickly. The next time I had sex, I was twenty-one and had done *lots* more research and advocacy work around sexuality and feminism, so I enjoyed it and focused as much on my pleasure (if not more on me than them)."

"A great experience I had with pleasure was when I had sex with my boyfriend at the time for the very first time. He had never had sex before, and it was special for him. I felt very happy being able to share that with him."

"I've had both. I actually found out how to find it at a young age, but because of what I heard, I always felt like a bad person for doing so."

"I've never really felt comfortable talking about my sexual experiences or how I feel on the topic. My mom has always said to hold off until marriage, but if I couldn't, talk to her about it. That's what scared me the most, I guess, having to tell my mom that I wanted to do that. I think I was also scared of never doing anything and being labeled as 'goody-two-shoes' or whatever. When I finally found someone that I wanted to do something with, I felt gross after because we had to hide and keep it a secret. We weren't dating, and he didn't care about me in the way I did about him. He was and is my only sexual encounter with another person, and I still felt like a 'hoe' for wanting and doing anything like that, I guess. Also with my friends being like "Don't drink after me or the same bottle as me anymore because you're gross now."

Chapter

4

Abortion

On the first day of my internship at a reproductive health center, I was given a tour and stepped into the abortion center. As I walked in, the waiting room was a calm environment. There was a TV for patients to watch any show of their choosing when feeling anxious, soft blankets, comfortable chairs, and notebooks for journaling entries.

"Those are for patients to write their stories in, why they're here essentially," my mentor said. Within the next few months, I would often end up in the waiting room with fellow coworkers flipping through the pages and digesting the stories. Each story was different—whether it was about financial instability, an unplanned pregnancy, an abusive partner, or age.

When reproductive health organizations and I were advocating for abortion access in the state of Rhode Island during this time, I wondered how we could anonymously voice the stories of those who had gotten an abortion so that they don't feel silenced or stigmatized by political leaders, protestors, and the list goes on. I soon decided to add a chapter about abortion in this book.

While advocating for abortion rights, I would like to emphasize that women are not the only people who get abortions. Abortion access affects folks of all identities. It's important to make this work as inclusive as possible, so let us begin now.

What would the world look like without stigma around abortion?

free
better
inclusive

What was your experience like getting an abortion?

"It was scary and traumatic. I felt really guilty, but I knew it was the right choice. I was letting the comments of 'abortion is murder' get to me, even though I knew it wasn't true. It's my body, my choice, and I know what is right/wrong. After the abortion, I did feel relieved, but I was still sad. I had this feeling of guilt, but I'm learning to work through it. I feel that if abortion wasn't so stigmatized, I would have felt better about my abortion and not so ashamed."

What was your experience like telling someone about your abortion?

"I felt almost ashamed in a way. It's something that is hard to talk about because I get scared people are going to think I am a terrible person. I want to keep it to myself, but at the same time I want to help other women who may be going through it."—Seventeen-year-old, Cis-female, Straight, From Providence, Rhode Island, She/Her/Hers Pronouns

"I have known *many* people who have had an abortion. The more I talk about abortion (try to destroy the stigma around it and create a safe space to talk about it), the more people open up to me about their own abortion. Storytelling is *vital* to destigmatization and a realistic depiction of what abortion is like for the people who experience them. I learned a lot through supporting my best friend through her 'empowered abortion,' which included her openly communicating with her two seven-year-olds what was happening when she took the pill at home and her photo documenting the process. Abortion is freedom."

Chapter

5

Birth Work

"More research and focus on specific challenges of black maternal healthcare."

"The midwifery model of care is a powerful tool for achieving reproductive justice and birth equity. The integration of midwifery into healthcare systems results in lower rates of Cesarean sections, preterm labor, low birth weight, and infant and maternal deaths. Despite a long history of midwifery in the black community, less than 5 percent of midwives in the United States are black. It is imperative that we have more black midwives and those specifically trained in alternative birth practices to help eliminate maternal mortality."

"Less than one year into my new position at a federally qualified health center (FQHC), the black maternal and infant mortality health crisis went from a cautionary tale of what happens in paternalistic healthcare systems to an emblematic reality in my daily life. I have witnessed three vibrant and determined postpartum mothers perish, two newborns lose the potential of their lives to sudden infant death syndrome (SIDS), and nearly half of our prenatal patient population suffer from maternal morbidity. Conducting chart reviews left me disoriented, disassociated, and almost numb as I reviewed one poor health outcome after another and closed the prenatal episodes of the deceased. The patients I memorialize above all had one thing in common—they were all black."

"Black women, birthing persons, and infants are at an increased risk of health inequities due to systemic racism perpetuated in healthcare. Every day at work, I witness our black prenatal patients reduced to their high-risk diagnosis, insurance status, demographic information, and vitals. I watch as our patients' wisdom, expertise, and multifaceted identities fail to become integrated into their clinical care. The disproportionate ratio of black providers to black prenatal patients, preconceived notions of patient accessibility, and the lack of care by a consistent provider are indicative of the racism, classism, and bias embedded in the culture of the FQHC. These practices and prejudices result in higher rates of underdiagnosing, fatal gaps in care, and mistrust."

"By the time a prenatal patient gets to my office for social support, they are already profoundly disappointed, frustrated, and suspicious of the institution I represent. For black women and birthing persons, the idea of a safe and autonomous birth appears increasingly elusive. To achieve maternal health equity, we must collectively struggle to address the bias and structural racism within our healthcare system."

"While I have not yet given birth, I have supported black women through birthing in the capacity of a doula. I would like to share a brief story regarding my first doula client. I have used an anonymous name for my client and their family.

"For hours I advocated against medical actions that threatened Deon's bodily autonomy. Nothing went according to the plan we spent weeks constructing together. I held her hand and continuously counseled her on her options. I requested new providers when doctors ignored her pain. In the end, I sat frustrated, hurt, tired, and confused as the surgical team wheeled them off for an unplanned C-section. Yet the biggest reward was that in the middle of a global pandemic, Deon; her mother, Monica; and her baby, Charity, were not alone. Every day, communities are engaging in structurally oppressive healthcare systems. The responsibility of advocacy sustained me as a doula at Deon's side and hovers over me as I continue to support black women and birthing persons through their pregnancy."

"Pregnancy is a lot. Enjoy your youth while you can because once you get pregnant, you have to make yourself ready to be a mom and a teenager at the same time and balance it, which can be very hard. And babies are not cheap either, so you better have a stable paycheck. You have to work, go to school, appointments, no drinking or smoking, no more parties, morning pills, and morning sickness."

"I had to learn to not sleep on my stomach. Braxton Hicks hurt, baby kicks hurt too, contractions hurt, and after birth, you are still in pain. It's a beautiful but painful journey."

"The fact that the rate of maternal mortality during childbirth is two to three times *higher* for black women than for white women is *absolutely* a result of implicit racism. Our system is failing women, but black women are especially vulnerable and targeted because they experience racism as well. We need to do better by, first and foremost, not being afraid to acknowledge and address it."

Chapter

6

Reproductive Advocacy

My experiences in reproductive advocacy and youth empowerment began at the root of my very first experiences in activism. On February 14, 2018, I was outside of the DEI center handing out flowers to members of the school who passed by. On this very same day, the Stoneman Douglas High School shooting occurred.

Within the following days, I attended a meeting with youth across Rhode Island as we wanted to make an impact by vocalizing the voices of those who have been impacted by gun violence personally or were scared of the possibility of a mass shooting. During the meeting, we discussed who would be making speeches at the State House. In 2018, I decided to help a friend of mine write her speech. In the following days that I was at my internship, something clicked. I realized that I could use my voice in a positive way and still make an impact as a young person. From that point on, I was canvassing with politicians, phone banking, volunteering at A coalition against gun violence, and writing testimonies about reducing gun violence.

Stepping into junior year, I established an internship at a reproductive health organization where I was teaching sex education. Within my very first few days, I met a community organizer. The bond was instantaneous, and we began to talk about how we could engage young people in political opportunities. Within the first few hours of meeting each other, we created an action plan. In November, our youth empowerment organization was born! I couldn't believe it—we founded a youth program. The remainder of the year was a whirlwind of experiences—zero supporters to hundred-plus supporters, Saturday meetings, menstrual drives, workshops, and then the Reproductive Health Care Act (RHCA) was released.

The RHCA would protect safe, legal abortion in Rhode Island if *Roe v. Wade* were to be overturned. Throughout my internship, I began to help prepare for long nights at the State House waiting for a vote and often attended rallies almost every week between January and May of 2019. At my first RHCA rally, I looked around and noticed that I was the only young person in the crowd of pink supporting abortion rights. *Why am I the only young person here?* I asked myself. I knew that this needed to change.

Within the following months, we engaged young people across Rhode Island to attend rallies at the State House, participate in phone banking, and write testimonies on why reproductive health care is vital to our futures. The day finally came—the RHCA was being voted on. I had been working at another job and could not attend, yet I kept my fingers crossed for the bill to be passed. As I was putting away supplies, I heard people behind me talk about how excited they were about the RHCA not being passed. This could not be right. I turned around and asked if the bill passed. "No!" and "I'm so happy!" were said from various people. I ran into the closet and cried continuously. I asked myself the following: *Was all of the time and energy working on that campaign worth it? Did I not try hard enough? Did we not try hard enough?* I contacted one of my mentors and said, "That's it, we're organizing a protest," and so we did.

I wanted the protest to be youth-led and to allow young folks to speak on behalf of their reproductive rights. With over sixty youth attendees and several speakers, we began to make a small impact. Of course, there were protestors yelling in our faces that we were "too young," "warped," and "only teenagers"; but that simply increased our resilience.

During the protest, an older man followed me around, stating that I was "brainwashed." Finally, I turned around and said, "I helped organize this protest." I witnessed his shocked facial expression, turned around, and kept walking. We as young people grew even stronger this day and never stopped advocating for our rights. After all, who better to lead our future than the people who are our future? I'll insert the link here for the article on the youth rally: https://upriseri.com/2019-05-24-repro-student-rally/.

To UpriseRI, thank you for writing this article. Adults at the State House remarked on how it was the largest youth turnout that they had seen in a long time. Soon after, the Reproductive Privacy Act (RPA) was released. The RPA was a duplicate of the RHCA and was brought to the senate for a larger vote. After several more weeks of rallies consisting of over 375 people, testimonies, and long hours at the State House—we did it! We passed the RPA! Abortion access is now protected in Rhode Island.

In August of 2019, a peer messaged me saying that while he was in Washington, DC, with other young activists. The group spoke about youth engagement in politics and used the work that I carried out for abortion access as an example toward a senator. One young woman remarked, "If one girl can make that big of an impact, then what can we do as a group of one hundred?" I nearly cried tears of joy. To all of the activists and advocates who consistently strive to change our earth and make it a better, more habitable place, you are doing great. Do not stop when it gets difficult.

What was your experience like advocating for reproductive rights?

"In 2017, my passion for political activism was initially sparked when I attended a social action conference in Washington, DC. Here, I learned about the world of public policy in greater depth than ever before. I was amazed by the power behind one individual's words and actions.
Among a variety of political topics, I studied reproductive rights. I was distraught when I learned that legislation protecting these freedoms was up for debate in my own state. Channeling my emotions into inspiration, I took action. I lobbied at the offices of my state senators and representatives, advocating for the protection of women's reproductive rights in Rhode Island.
I have since continued to express my political beliefs and speak up for positive change. With excitement and honor, I have spoken at multiple press conferences at the Rhode Island State House, actively expressing my passion toward this crucial freedom. In June 2019, a great success was achieved when the Reproductive Privacy Act was passed, protecting a woman's right to access reproductive healthcare. I find both pride and gratitude toward being so involved in the influential movement that pushed this act into law."

"Through my political activism, I have flourished, discovering my own power as a young woman. As I channel my own values, I am able to find enjoyment and success in making my voice heard. I love utilizing my passion in such a powerful way, with hopes that I positively impact others through advocating for access, equality, and justice."

"Informative, empowering, and frustrating at times (plus the classic religion-based harassment)."

"Best fight of my life."

What is one thing you'd like to tell legislators who attempt to strip away reproductive health rights?

"Reproductive rights are inevitable, and the future will reflect that. How do you want to be remembered? On which side of history?"

"I would like to tell legislators that these reproductive health rights are absolutely essential in keeping people healthy and safe. Out of respect for the women of our country, we must keep reproductive healthcare easily accessible to all."

"Reproductive rights are inalienable rights."

"F——ck off."

What feelings did you experience when advocating for reproductive health?

"As a young woman, I have felt unsafe and unprotected in the past as the topic of reproductive health has become heavily debated. When I became aware that my own state was debating legislation to protect such freedoms, I felt even more vulnerable and unsafe. I felt the pressing need to take some type of action, so I eagerly spoke at the Rhode Island State House at a press conference, advocating for the Reproductive Privacy Act. It was passed a few months later, therefore ensuring and protecting a woman's right to access reproductive healthcare across the state. I felt great pride toward being a part of the influential movement that pushed this act into law. Advocating for reproductive healthcare enabled me to find the most empowered, confident, and passionate version of myself. By becoming involved in political activism, specifically reproductive health, I have gained confidence and found meaning in my advocacy for such important rights."

"Frustration, exhaustion, empowerment, ferocity, moral certainty."

"The city of Baltimore is 62 percent black and 53 percent female. The poverty rate in Baltimore is 22 percent, and this rate is significantly higher for people from historically marginalized groups. On a warm day in February, I was walking with my husband in the Inner Harbor when we witnessed a group of people protesting In a city where the majority of the population is black + female, these protestors were all white + male. Blood boiling. I approached a protestor + asked him if he knew that a reproductive health center provides healthcare services *beyond abortion* to the city's most vulnerable children + families. I was enraged that these men—who have no business commenting on women's health issues—had such a distorted, singular view. I made this perfectly clear, felt excellent about my monthly donations to a reproductive health center + walked away from toxic masculinity, racism, and ignorance."

"Through my social activism, specifically reproductive advocacy, I have formed countless meaningful relationships with other equally passionate individuals. I am grateful to have found such confident, resilient, and vibrant people who find equal importance in such topics."

"I've seen a lot of pro-life friends saying things along the lines of 'My body, my choice? Last I checked, the human body didn't have two hearts and four arms' (which, like, correct, glad we all passed Health and Anatomy 101). However, that's not what my body, my choice means! I've got an analogy for you (I saw this online and can't remember where it's from, but creds to whoever came up with this!). Imagine you're at the hospital and someone desperately needs a blood transfusion. You're type O negative, so you could donate your blood. Would you? Probably. But can the doctors force you to? Definitely not. If they end up dying, are you liable? No. Because your blood is a part of *your* body. Thanks to bodily autonomy, we as humans have the right to govern what we give and don't give of our bodies to anyone else, even if it results in someone else's death. So my body, my choice is not saying that the fetus is a part of my body, therefore I can do what I want with it. My body, my choice is simply saying that the fetus is no more entitled to my body than anyone else is."

Chapter

7

Teen Pregnancy

What were some of the challenges you faced while being pregnant as a teenager?

"People looking at me and telling me that my life is over."

"Some challenges for me were people staring at me, missing school, or making enough money to get ready for my bundle of joy."

What was your experience like sharing with others that you were pregnant as a teenager?

"It was a relief, and I wasn't ashamed."

"It was actually nice. My friends and peers were happy and supportive of my choice."

What advice might you have for other pregnant teenagers?

"You're going to be a great mother or father. Don't let people tell you that you are going to fail or your life is over. It's only the beginning of a new life with your little one."

"I was depressed and scared for the first four months of my pregnancy. My baby's father was nowhere to be found, and he would not answer my texts. He blocked me on everything. Even after him not being there, my friends and family all supported me with love and kindness. I gained so much confidence throughout the next five months of being pregnant. Ever since I gave birth, I am lost for words that I actually created a human being that is handsome and full of joy and happiness."

"From mid-October to early November, I went through something scary. I had a pregnancy scare. Yes, I know to some it's not a scare, but scary or not, it's a big deal, once you really know more about it. I'm gonna say this right now—I didn't know enough. My middle school never talked to us about sex or enough about our bodies. My boyfriend and I didn't know we could get pregnant through this whole experience. He was here with me, and also through this, our relationship was a little bumpy, but we got through it. He told me we would be okay and I wouldn't lose him and he wouldn't lose me. The weekend of my birthday, he came over to celebrate with me and my family. When we had our alone time, we played around for a bit. He rubbed pre-cum on my private area, and he and I can't remember if he stuck it in me, but he did rub it on me. When he left, I got curious if pre-cum can make you pregnant. I googled it, and it said it couldn't, but there is a chance it can. That's where I got nervous. Then on Monday when I went back to school, I asked my friend, and he said it can and that he learned it from his middle school. That's when my fear really started to kick in. I didn't know anything, and I was scared, and I stressed myself out. It was just a horrible experience, and every day I would check if I got my period, and when the days went by, I was getting ready to tell someone, so I told my best friend. She said she would help me and get me a pregnancy test if I didn't get my period, but two days later, I got my period, but I was still nervous because I know if I don't get my second period, there's something wrong. But the next month I got my period, and ever since then, my period has come on time, which I am so thankful for."

Chapter

8

Toxic Masculinity

How could we change the culture that promotes toxic masculinity?

"Show more depictions of men safely expressing a wide range of emotions healthily (besides just anger and frustration); stop suppressing femininity; celebrate male softness rather than hardness/stoicism; create spaces for men to discuss their relationships, feelings, confusing life situations with their other male friends; destroy white heteropatriarchy; prioritize compassion, kindness, altruism, love, etc., instead of power, strength, wealth; teach men about women's incredible abilities, worth, and strength outside of them and to define being a good man (in part) by how much they support the women on their journey to be their most independent and strong selves rather than by their ownership of women as objects and wealth."

"Finally actively dismiss and denounce the aspects of our culture that glorify and reward the display of it, while encouraging and nurturing the creation of media, places, and people who allow the next generation to have the freedom to choose to be better without having to sacrifice so much of themselves as a caveat for not fitting the norm."

"We could work as a community to show men that it is normal to show their emotions."

"Accepting emotions and differences."

"We shouldn't stereotype colors or hygiene because all you're doing is taking care of yourself and like what you like."

"By teaching our sons not only how to respect the opposite gender and otherwise but also to support other men without it being labeled gay."

"Teach both males and females that we are equal and if we want something to change, we have to be the change. Don't do what you wouldn't want done to you."

"Eliminate gender stereotypes as a whole. Stop marketing toys as for boys/girls, stop assigning colors to genders, stop shaming men for taking part in 'feminine' activities and vice versa."

What is an experience that you've had with toxic masculinity?

"Once when I was sleeping over at my stepbrother's mom's house with him and his guy friend, his friend didn't think it was cool to hang out with and be kind to girls. I was told I could not play basketball with them and to draw on the sidelines. His friend was trying to prove/perform his masculinity by throwing the basketball at me, and he pressured my stepbrother to do the same to show that he was 'one of the guys.' My stepbrother always liked playing with me when no other boys were around (we shared a room and played together every day), but that day he agreed completely with his friend and spent the day throwing basketballs at me until I cried enough and ran inside. He was always nice to be with unless his guy friends were around, then all of a sudden, he couldn't stand me and had no kind feelings toward me."

"My father was mentally and verbally abusive toward us and didn't show much emotion, just anger."

"The one that sticks out most in my mind is of a friend from high school who was being pressured into sex by his girlfriend, and he was vulnerable enough to express this to me and some others. Many of the people he talked to completely dismissed his feelings on it and claimed he should feel 'lucky.' It was a very sickening display of people completely ignoring what was essentially a cry for help from an abusive relationship because they couldn't contemplate a world where anything was more important than getting their rocks off."

"I grew up with a sexist father who shamed everything (including me and my sister) that was feminine."

"I can't wear certain things. I'm judged for simply washing my face or taking on a certain job."

"Being pushed and bullied by my older cousins in order to 'toughen me up' and also having a gun pulled on me to do that same thing."

"Some guy told me 'women belong on their knees and in the kitchen.' And if they want equality, if a girl hits me, I'm going to hit them back."

"I worked in physical labor/mechanics, and many men assumed that I didn't know how to do my job."

"Being taught not to give 'too much' respect to a female because then they'll walk over you or take you for granted, therefore teaching me to keep all women at arm's length."

"Another guy said women who wear makeup and revealing clothes are asking to be touched and catcalled."

Chapter

9

Body Image

While talking about body image may not seem taboo, it can be. We often bring it up in conversations, post or see posts about it on social media platforms, and more. Yet the question is, are we really honest and open about it? Do we hold back in regard to talking about our insecurities? Do we open up the space for people to share their experiences enough? Whether it be through conversations, social media, and so forth, we can easily be fed ideas that lead us as a society to struggle with body image. Loving yourself and your body can take time and even be hard.

I myself struggled with body image from as young as elementary school. I was always on the smaller scale. As time progressed, my doctors grew concerned about how much my weight would fluctuate and realized that there could be a potential problem. I was soon referred to an endocrinologist who would monitor my weight and height. I was always at doctors' appointments, getting blood tests done, and spent countless hours at hospitals running tests just to figure out what was wrong.

I was eventually diagnosed with a growth hormone deficiency, and it certainly did not get easier from there. In seventh grade, I started growth hormone injections that I did every night before bed for over a year. I remember that during this time, I became so much more aware about being short or underweight that it was almost always what ran through my mind. While going through this process, I was later diagnosed with severe depression and anxiety, which certainly took an even larger toll on not only my body itself, but my body image. I grew increasingly insecure, dealt with self-harm, wore baggier clothing, and more. Due to the depression and anxiety, I succumbed to having issues with overeating, or not eating enough.

It wasn't until high school that I gained a very strong support system and began to make steps toward healing, taking care of myself better, and focusing on what I wanted to improve. It was very hard, and it was a long road to reach the point of where I am now of being comfortable in my skin and making healthy adjustments. By upholding conversations and sharing stories about body image, that counts as making one more step toward reducing the stigma and discomfort around the topic. Let's continue those efforts.

Short Shorts

> my brain cannot go the course
> I don't want to hear your whistles as I walk down the street
> my outfit is not a reason for you to mistreat me
> I'm so glad you love my outfit but your mouth seems to be full of bullshit
> and oh how could I forget about those shouts
> they ring through my head as I wander about
> I don't post pictures for clout

the amount of times I've been told this I cannot count
most women in the US have been harassed without doubt
I've been told I'll be a woman when I use my own mouth
hopefully they're thinking of when I start to shout
I am not your little doll
you cannot pick me up as you please
I don't like it when you tell me, "You'd look better on my knees"
please don't touch me, I didn't ask for that squeeze.
me wearing a crop top is not me being a tease
I'm sorry, I'm sorry I forgot how to breathe
in, out
in, out
oh kinda like the shouts
but some days I just like to look at the clouds
and when I fall asleep I count the sheep
did I say sheep I mean creeps
when I walk down Broad the comments come in heaps
and Nicki Minaj told me I'm for keeps
but who's keeping me when I hear those beeps
those beeps are not safe
no, I don't want your wave
my mom tells me to be brave
but these short shorts could dig my grave.

Has social media impacted your perception of body image? How so?

"So much. In the 90s and early 2000s, we had fashion and teen magazines. Now there is social media touting a curated idea of perfection. However, the other positive side to that is that social media is media that is created by the public and our peers. Therefore, there have been huge movements around body positivity and anti-diet culture and toxic body image that have also affected my perception of body image positively."

"Yes, it seems that people on social media are talking about their bodies, how they move them, what they put in them, what they love about them, what they hate about them constantly. The constant talk and discussion and attention on body image makes it really hard to try to accept the one you have."

"Sometimes it makes me think that I should be skinnier. When I see all these pictures of famous women that are so gorgeous and shaped perfectly, it makes me want the same sometimes."

"Certainly it has. Social media is constantly bombarding you with ideas of what the ideal body is and how to get it. What I think is so hypocritical about that is that whatever the 'ideal' body is always changes. Every few years beauty standards shift, sometimes dramatically, and yet people are still shamed when they don't fit the current bill."

"Yes. Social media puts out negative energy and stigma surrounding certain body types. But it forces you to deal with it head-on. It's a pro and con situation."

"Yes, I've always used social media as a tool of my own destruction. Comparison is dangerous to the teenage psyche, and you end up falling down a rabbit hole of self-doubt. I have struggled with an eating disorder, specifically anorexia, for about a year now, and seeing the 'thinspo' and 'fitspo' pushed me to fit myself into a tiny box and an even tinier body."

"Yes, it makes me feel like I'm not pretty enough and that I'm not slim enough."

"Every app I open, often the first thing I see is a picture of someone who I perceive as 'beautiful.' Whether it be a famous celebrity, a model, or even something as innocent as an advertisement, sometimes it seems there is nothing I can do to silence the voice in the back of my brain that is constantly comparing me to these pictures. What society perceives as 'beautiful' or 'attractive' is only what is trending online, and it has forced me to try to reach those standards in my reality; however, whenever I don't reach my own pressured standards, I feel disappointed, and even ugly."

"Yesss, there are some posts that make me comfortable and proud of my body, but then there are others that make me feel not so good about myself."

"Oh definitely, growing up in a time where social media was such a big part of culture had a lot to do with it. You always had to look the best and seem the happiest. At first, nobody cared, but suddenly the number of likes and comments was a big factor. Then there were the girls that had the slim waist, big butts, and big boobs that started to slowly get to you. You make the connections and overthink. Social media has made me feel like I had to have a certain body and if I didn't or couldn't, I wasn't enough."

"Definitely, I have seen lots of popular advertising with muscular white men. This may not personally make me feel bad, but it has made lots of people that are on social media—some of which I know—very self-aware."

"A little bit. At first, I thought that I had to look a certain way, and because of that stigma, I lost a lot of confidence within myself."

"Yes, I see so many beautiful people with the body that I want, and it makes me so sad and insecure. When I see other women with my ideal body, I can't help but think that I should starve myself even though I know it's wrong."

"Of course. 'Thinspo' or 'thinspiration' is found all over social media, and it's not hard to be drawn into that sort of community. I've also noticed that I can get lost in pictures of these dangerously thin women and feel like shit after I do. Social media is a great thing, but sometimes it really, really sucks, especially if you're trying to recover from an eating disorder."

What would the world look like if there was more body positivity?

"There wouldn't be so many girls with depression and anxiety. We would feel more free to be ourselves instead of trying to impress others."

"More confidence in myself. People showing up authentically."

"I'm not sure body positivity is what we need to be working toward. In an ideal world, body neutrality would be the goal. I had a friend once tell me that when she gets obsessed over her body, she thinks, *There are so many more interesting things about me than my body and how I look.* When I first heard that, I rolled my eyes because growing up plus size, I was always judged because of my size; my whole identity was tied to how my body looked, so that idea seemed almost impossible. But after doing some work on unpacking internalized fatphobia and figuring out my identity, I realized she's right."

"I would like to think people would feel more comfortable living as they are and engage in a lot less self-destructive behavior that unfortunately harms so many lives. I think an obstacle to this is it's very much one of those things that everyone needs to be on board for and encouraging. If enough people refuse to be accepting, it's going to be so much harder for people to accept themselves."

"I think that people wouldn't think twice about putting themselves into new situations. I think that positivity is the new criticism. Instead of bringing suggestions to the table of how to lose weight or how to look better, we should be praising the natural body how it is, the healthy body."

"If the world was more body-positive, it would mean that a lot more teenagers specifically could get out of their shell and interact with their fellow peers instead of living with fear and disgust with how they look. The teenage years are the harshest for anybody, and if they're also dealing with self-image problems because of their body, it makes it even worse."

"I honestly think that the world in general would be a more accepting and free place."

"Beautiful."

"If the world was more accepting of all body types and faces, so many young people would not feel discouraged every time they looked down at their cell phone or walked by peers in the halls. Anxiety caused by insecurities would reduce, and more people would feel comfortable in their own skin and have the ability to be themselves. Instead of the silence and self-hatred that so many allow themselves to endure, the world would be more harmonized because people would be lifting each other up."

"The world would be more positive and people would feel comfortable and support each other."

"Happier. I think everyone would be more content with themselves and with that more content with others."

"I think that society would be less demanding, and there would be so many people who can live happily no matter what physical situation they are in."

"The world would be such a better place and all-inclusive to everyone's body shape."

"So many more people would be happier and healthier. No one would have to worry if they look fat in their jeans or if their nose is too big or even if they don't have the abs of a bodybuilder."

"Another guy said women who wear makeup and revealing clothes are asking to be touched and catcalled."

"I think people would be happier. People could wear what they wanted to without constantly worrying about what their body looks like. It would also save *so* much time, no more thinking about what to wear, just dressing how you feel."

"Diversity! Variety! Reality! Flavor!"

"Better. With no judgment."

"The world would have peace."

"Less eating disorders and hatred for our bodies; the beauty industry would be worth a lot less; advertising wouldn't focus on what is wrong with you but would celebrate our differences and realities."

How has having an eating disorder affected your health?

"I happened to have an eating disorder right around the time I started birth control, and my hormones were extremely out of order. I don't have periods, and I'm still unsure whether it's the ED or the birth control. Having an ED means you're usually freezing and exhausted. I miss being able to go on walks without needing to sit five minutes in. I am severely anorexic, and I'm on the road to recovery."

"It's put me in and out of hospitals since I was twelve."

"I have phases where I eat a lot and think about food 24/7 and other phases where I barely eat and feel good about myself. When I eat a lot, I feel trapped and superguilty. I think that this has affected more my psychological health and my physical health."

"I don't have a diagnosed eating disorder, but I think the fact that I and many people I know are shamed or gawked at just for eating when we are hungry speaks volumes about the general attitude around food and its consumption in America. I've always been of the belief that if you're hungry, you should eat. Plain and simple. It's your body's way of telling you to eat, and the fact we are often encouraged to ignore that or substitute for it (just drink water instead, sleep it off, etc.) is incredibly unhealthy and sad to see."

"A few months back, I can remember when I started losing weight. I knew I wasn't happy with myself, but I was finally glad that I started seeing results from days of not eating enough or not eating at all. In addition to this, I started exercising almost every day, which only made me feel tremendously fatigued 24/7. While on a school trip to Florida, I remember staying up later than everyone else in my hotel room because I was so nauseous from not eating and my stomach would be rumbling. When I would wake up, everyone wanted to go get breakfast, and I felt so disgusted with myself for eating just the one yogurt with fruit that held me over for the entire day in the ninety-degree heat. After losing almost thirty pounds in a little under a month, I started to realize that it was a serious problem and finally opened up to a few of my closest friends. Not only did this have a negative impact on my physical health, but to this day, I still struggle with the anxieties of not being enough for anyone because I don't have the body of a Victoria's Secret model. Eating disorders can be linked to depression, something I am also still struggling with to this day, but I can happily say that I've been steadily gaining weight back and am making the honest effort to eat more healthy foods that are rich in proteins and nutrients."

"I used to have a binging and purging eating disorder which caused me to have stomach problems and weakened my mental health stability. Sometimes I can't think things through all the way without overthinking my decisions, or I just lose interest on things and focus on what I need to consume."

"I was never diagnosed with an eating disorder, but I did suffer from restrictive eating. It made me worse, getting to a level in which I didn't believe I deserved food."—Fifteen-year-old, Cis-female

"My eating disorder made me cold all the time. It's made me have headaches and missed periods. I almost always feel tired. And the worst part is sometimes I don't see anything wrong with it—I think it's good. I'm trying to get out of that mindset, but once you have an ED, it's super hard to get rid of."

"Negatively. I've lost some friends, and I almost killed myself in the process. I also could never leave the house because I was always cold. I'm still having trouble with anorexia, and I weigh myself seven times every day. Now I have gotten rid of my scale. At the doctors, I prefer not to weigh myself as it's a trigger for me."

"I hated my body and thought I was ugly starting at age twelve and also thought that there was an ideal body type and I certainly didn't have it. I never had an eating disorder, but I have always had disordered eating habits and had a *very* unhealthy relationship with food throughout my high school years (exercise as punishment and healthy food to avoid being ugly/fat, hated myself when I enjoyed food that was considered bad/fattening). Most people have negative body images and unhealthy relationships with their body/food/exercise, but particularly girls. By age ten, about 80 percent of girls have tried a diet, and that is a direct result of our culture."

"I used to be called fat and ugly because of my weight in middle school and in high school as well when I went to my old school. I already had depression and anxiety, but when I felt so confident and beautiful one day, this boy from my old school told me that I was fat, and hearing that gave me so much anxiety that everyone was looking at me thinking I am fat and ugly."

"An experience I've had with body image was that people used to tell me that I was too skinny, that I have to gain weight, I'm not strong, I can't fight, etc. Honestly, for a while I felt self-conscious about my body type. I felt the need to start working out to gain muscles and weight. Then I started to realize that

I shouldn't care about what others think about my own body! God made me like this so I will be proud of my slimmer fit. I do still want to gain weight and exercise, to be honest. But I no longer need to get approval from others on how I should look, but instead because I want to do it."

"People don't realize the impact that comments can have on a person. From that day on, I've struggled with disordered eating, and I'm starting to recover now. While I do feel stronger now, there are still days where I relapse and use unhealthy coping mechanisms as a means of trying to look thinner, and I have faced the medical complications of doing so. Moral of the story: *don't* comment on what people are eating!"

"Body image seemed to have always been a big deal to me. It was this mind game I continued to play and entertain. I'd go from feeling amazing about myself and the way I looked to hating every curve and edge. To this day, it's a thing I struggle with, and that's not to say it doesn't get better and easier because I am definitely not at the same spot I was a year ago with it. It just takes time to refocus yourself, and life is about new experiences and perspectives. Nobody is just alike, and neither are their stories because if they were, life would be boring in itself."

"Growing up as a chubby cis-male, there were many times where you could end up being the butt of a joke, and it was all in good fun until it wasn't. There's a limit where the jokes stop being funny and you start questioning your self-worth. When you reach your limit, you reach a point where you either have the drive to change yourself or stay the same. I chose to change, and I'm glad I did. The level of confidence and power that comes with it is unmatched."

"I grew up as a tall, skinny, white, blue-eyed male. I have definitely had the benefit of looking the way I do, but even I have been made fun of for being so skinny. Even though I was never really hurt by how others judged me, it does not mean it is okay."

"I've always been so insecure of my body because I've always been the biggest girl in the room. I was bullied in elementary school for it, and I hated coming to school just to see the people who made me want to cry in the middle of class."

Chapter

10

LGBTQIA+ Experiences

In May 2018, I spoke on a youth panel for a youth sexual health education conference. During youth panel meetings, the group and I discussed the impact of what non-inclusive environments have on members of the LGBTQ+ community. This conversation made it especially apparent that the healthcare system still discriminates against people who identify as LGBTQ+, struggles to assist their needs, or fails to provide a safe space. How are folks expected to freely address their healthcare needs when feeling judged by providers? Together, we can make spaces more inclusive by putting in the work. While sitting on the panel, other young people and I spoke about our experiences at the doctors to statewide health providers. I shared this one particular story about how almost every time I've met with a doctor, they ask if I'm sexually active. Although this is a common question, it's always about "using a condom for protection." It can be quite awkward being asked this question when you're in a relationship with the same gender! Especially when the patient themselves have to address it. Instead, providers can ask questions such as "What methods are you using to prevent pregnancy and STIs?" "What are you using as birth control, if any?" or even just asking simple questions about the patient's partner. It was great to hear providers respond by asking us questions related to how they can best modify their practices and open up the spaces around them to feel more comfortable and safe. This is why we need these conversations to happen. This is what helps us make progress. This is what helps break the stigma.

What would the world look like without stigma toward the LGBTQ+ community (one-word answer)?

beautiful
equal
peaceful
happier
rainbow
colorful

AUDREY LEE O'DONNELL

Can you tell me about your experience as a member of the LGBTQ+ community in the world?

"My experience being LBGTQ+ hasn't been easy, but I guess no one's really has. My mom was supportive of LGBTQ+ people, but that was before I came out. Every time we talk, she brings it up—how I'm making a mistake by transitioning, how I'm ruining my life, etc. But thanks to hormones, I'm no longer uncomfortable with my body and my appearance. When I look at myself in the mirror, the person I see 1,000 percent reflects the person I know I was supposed to become.

When I identified as female, I'd look in the mirror, and I wouldn't recognize the person looking back at me, and it was severely disorienting seeing a stranger in the mirror every day. When my (female) puberty started, I began having breakdowns over my body. My mind just didn't connect with my body. I ended up developing an eating disorder, almost as a way to slow my body's puberty down.

When I moved to Rhode Island, I decided to transition. I cut off all my hair and asked everyone around me to call me by a different name. I came out to my mom, and she laughed at me, saying that I couldn't possibly be a boy because I played with dolls as a kid (but I also refused to wear dresses and exclusively watched superhero movies). My stepdad mocked me and would belittle me and other transgender people constantly.

When I was in eighth grade (the same year I came out), my sisters and I were placed in foster care. I hated it at first, but then I realized that all the new adults in my life were incredibly supportive of my identity. We began the long fight for me to start hormones. The only thing was that we needed my mom's consent in order for me to start, but when she wouldn't consent, we opted for a different route. We took my mom to court (multiple times), but in order for me to start hormones and for my sisters to get adopted, we had to terminate her parental rights. After that, I was able to start hormones right before I turned sixteen, which is pretty rare for transgender youth.

Although I no longer identify as a trans male, I still align with masculinity more so than femininity. I currently identify as nonbinary, but that can always change as humans are naturally very fluid beings. I've come to a point in my transition where I feel comfortable enough embracing both masculine and feminine energies. But if it wasn't for hormones, I wouldn't be at this level of comfort with my body. I'd still be battling with gender dysphoria and probably many more problems."

"I started questioning my sexuality at fourteen. I lived in an accepting area (Bay Area) and knew many gay and lesbian people, some bisexuals, and had met a few trans people. But I didn't think any of those labels fit me, so it wasn't until twenty-one that I came out to myself as pansexual, then quickly the rest of the world. It was a confusing journey, but I'm so grateful that I always found myself intertwined in the queer community and fighting alongside many activists. That being said, as a pansexual, I often have not (and still don't) felt very seen or respected by my own community, as a woman and as a pansexual. It's difficult to be in a minority within a minority, but also experience privilege (as a white woman who passes as straight with my cis-male partner). That being said, I also often feel like I am misjudged as a straight woman when I'm in queer spaces and feel very unwelcome, which can be tricky. I have found some amazing people in the community that support me though, and the closest people around me tend to also be some flavor of queer. Even with its challenges, I would never want to be straight."

"Living in Rhode Island, I haven't dealt with much hate, but there have been a few instances right around after I cut my hair very short. I have been called a fag, a dyke, and a "queer" by people standing or sitting near me for no apparent reason. I also went into the men's restroom one time, and as I was coming out the door, I felt so accomplished, but then a man waiting looked at me, disgusted, rolled his eyes, and walked away, and that one probably hurt the most. I know that I am stronger and smarter than them, though."

"I haven't been discriminated against by most people, yet I was harassed by somebody after I came out. I hear slurs nearly every day."

"Whenever I tell someone my sexuality, they always ask the same sentence, "You don't look gay.""

"It's been good and bad—good that I can be myself around the people I love and bad that I sometimes get judged for my sexual preference by guys."

"When I was younger, I never really cared for the gay and straight topics. Then I started having feelings for other girls, but I didn't understand them in a romantic way. Once I got to middle school, I would google sexuality and gender and explored my own. I had many 'phases' thinking maybe I could be lesbian, bi, or trans, or even nonbinary. It was a confusing time, and I was heavily bullied for dating girls and identifying as nonbinary, and that drove me into a deep depression and low self-worth. I experienced so much homophobia I started to think it was normal. After putting up with the mistreatment for almost two years, I became very suicidal and would self-harm, and I wanted to kill myself. Every day I had to face my tormentors was a day I fell deeper down the rabbit hole of sadness and fear. Finally I got help from a therapist after my school called my mom when my friend told a teacher that I wanted to kill myself. From that experience, I am left with so much fear and am scared when I hold my partner's hand or think of getting married. I'm always afraid I won't be able to find love."

"Mostly positive, but at some points feeling a stigma toward how I act/present myself."

"I've been lucky enough to grow up in a fairly progressive town/family. However, certain people in my life claim to be oh so accepting until it's someone they know."

How has being a member of the LGBTQ+ community affected your ability in accessing healthcare?

"Because I am white, cis, mostly gender conforming, and straight passing, I don't think I have experienced any additional barriers to healthcare access because of my sexuality (just the typical financial restrictions to access)."

"I don't really deal with those kinds of things, but it took a lot of persuading to convince my parents to let me go to the gender clinic at a Children's Hospital in Rhode Island."—Fourteen-year-old, Gender Fluid/Nonbinary Trans, Queer, They/Them/Theirs Pronouns

"I don't tell any healthcare professionals that I'm a member of the LGBTQ+ community for fear of discrimination."

"It's been very odd, going to an all-girls school and being the only one in the whole high school (as far as I know) who doesn't identify as female. Most have been supportive, and a lot of people have been very confused, and we really need to educate all children on gender identity, starting at a young age, so that in the future, kids like me don't have to explain themselves all the time."

"Whenever I'm with someone else who is also a part of the community and physically out that they are gay, they get all the rude looks and eye rolls. It's just infuriating to me that people are this way."

Chapter

11

Birth Control

What kind of implications do you think the gag rule will have on people accessing birth control?

"Less access to education and information; lower understanding of options and compassion for teen pregnancies and STIs; more unplanned/unwanted pregnancies; higher gender pay gap; women learning less personal autonomy early in their life; stall progress in feminist movement; perpetuating fear/damaging myths around sex and pleasure."

"It won't stop teens from having sex. It will only lead to more unplanned pregnancies."

"Teens will face unwanted pregnancies, and some of them will either raise unloved, unwanted, and neglected children or won't raise that child at all. They may put them in foster care even though the system is already so full and can't possibly be the best choice for that child. And some teens may try to have a back-alley abortion or their bodies may not be ready for birthing and they could die."

"Without access to birth control, many women and teens will be left with no choice but to resort to possible abortions or unsafe sex. If people want to stop abortions, they should make birth control normal, not a stigma."

"The gag rule would mean that women, teenage women included, may no longer have full access to and understanding of their options when it comes to birth control, which could easily mean an increase in unplanned pregnancies, and make it less likely that women will know how to obtain a safe and legal abortion if they so choose. It sets the clock back on women making progress toward equal rights and access to healthcare in this country and puts both mothers and children at increased and unnecessary medical risk. Further, providers will now be faced with a choice to either stop providing or talking about abortion or no longer receive Title X funds, which could force them to cut back on services or even have to close down. The loss of services like reproductive health centers would further impact both the physical and mental health of countless women in this country, myself included. Abortions will always continue to happen no matter what the laws say, and banning appropriate counseling around abortion will do nothing but lead to an increase in unsafe abortions. Teens especially will be more likely to seek out unsafe/illegal contraception or abortion methods, placing them at serious risk of harm or death."

What was your experience like accessing birth control?

"I am very privileged and have always had access to birth control (always lived close to PP, have always had insurance that I could get it through, my feminist mother is extremely enthusiastic about getting me birth control whenever I wanted it). I have been on hormonal birth control for a time in the past, and have always been able to buy condoms and Plan B when needed or desired."

"After my mom found an unused condom in the washing machine, she said that I should probably start birth control because condoms aren't always 100 percent effective. I was really relieved because I had recently had a pregnancy scare, but I was really nervous to ask her about it. I got a prescription from my doctor for Sprintec, which is a type of birth control pill. At first, I got it from my pharmacy, but then I learned about the Pill Club, a monthly subscription that mails you birth control, Plan B, and a bunch of bonus goodies. It made it much, much easier to access what I needed, so I preach about it to everyone I know!"

"I was lucky enough to have a mother who spoke with me frankly about sex and birth control starting at a young age, and she took me to the gynecologist to get started on oral contraceptives at age sixteen, no questions asked. Unfortunately, the doctor was quite stigmatizing, and my experience with that medical provider triggered a several-years-long struggle with anxiety when going to the physician that lasted nearly into my thirties. It was not until I decided to start going to a reproductive health center that I truly felt heard and not at all ashamed about my sexuality and contraceptive choices (including being a now-thirty-five-year-old woman who prefers to live child-free), and as a result, I was able to finally make well-informed decisions for myself (like getting an IUD, which has been amazing—I'm six years period-free and don't have to worry about getting pregnant!), and my anxiety around going to the doctor has finally improved."

"Ever since becoming sexually active, I wanted to start birth control. Condoms are very uncomfortable for me, but I didn't want to get pregnant, so I decided to finally get on the pill after being persuaded by girlfriends who were also on it. I went to a reproductive health center and got it for free, and I was excited to start. Birth control has done wonderful things for me, not only to prevent pregnancy, but reduced period cramps and shortened my periods. It has only made me throw up once, and it didn't make me gain a ton of weight. I was so scared to tell my family about it, but once I told my sister, I felt better because she talked to me about how she was on it before too. I was scared to tell my mom most of all and didn't want her to find out in the first place. Once she found out, she was surprisingly accepting of it. Getting on birth control is something that nobody should be ashamed of. It's making the right choice for you to remain safe from pregnancy and other things."

"Birth control is *life-changing*, and everyone who wants it should have access (also, there needs to be a male hormonal birth control option). But it should not be used as a one-size-fits-all for menstrual pain/problems. There needs to be more medical research into both menstrual pain *and* birth control's long-term effects on things like fertility and ways to regulate the reproductive system without the very uncomfortable side effects that uterus owners disproportionately have to suffer to prevent pregnancy."

Chapter

12

Domestic Violence and Sexual Assault

What was your experience like when asking or seeking help?

"I was not respected, understood, or believed that I was in a relationship with the abuser. I had to see him at school every day. I was belittled and called a wh——re and sl——t constantly by his friends. It trained my brain to accept bad behavior because every time that I told someone, they would just ignore the problem. The teachers would tell me that it wasn't okay, and then they did nothing about it. He was supermanipulative and pushed me to do things sexually I was not comfortable with. This happened repeatedly until I left. But even when I left, it wasn't because he was abusive; it was because I wasn't getting enough attention. So I guess afterward I still had to go to school, and I didn't think it was bad to begin with. I just had all of this pent-up anger, and I didn't understand it because my mind and body had blocked out the trauma until a year later once I finally realized what was happening. I am diagnosed now with PTSD. I switched schools three times, but nothing seemed to work. I felt alone, and no one completely understood what I was going through no matter how many times I explained it. So now because of that, I had to be admitted into the hospital. I got really suicidal, and I was struggling to keep living. When I stayed overnight in an inpatient, I was then shamed for my trauma. Then in an outpatient, I finally got people who understood and made me feel safe and recognize it isn't my fault. I am stronger now and am working to get better, and I am day by day. I learned that healing isn't linear, and what happened to me is in the past, and I can now move forward to greater and bigger things."

"I reported sexual harassment to the administrative team at my school when it happened. None of them believed me."

"I was terrified. I was so scared that somehow the situation would be turned on me. I was scared that it was my fault. That something I did made this man do this to me. I was scared to say something; it would ruin his life. He had a family. I was scared for them. What would his daughter say when she found out what her father had done? These thoughts and fears consumed me. Should I say something? I knew my words would not be taken lightly. Should I stay silent? Maybe it would just be easier. However, the easy option was not the right option, and I knew that. I would not let this man to this to another young girl. No fifteen-year-old should ever battle with this. No fifteen-year-old should have to endure something so damaging. I would not be silenced."

"When I sought help, most people I encountered were willing to help, as I think they all believed me and knew that the right thing to do would be to help me. But they all treated it as if it were a huge burden and seemed annoyed/mad at me for bringing it up. There was just a general sense of exhaustion and that all they were doing wasn't really worth it. It made me feel really ashamed and like what happened wasn't worthy of looking for help. Every time I told the story again, I purposefully used less and less detail because it seemed like that's what they wanted, and I regret not telling the full story now."

"I was met with comments like 'You can handle it' or 'Just leave her' or something of the equivalent."

"I was too scared to ever ask for help."

"I was too scared to tell my story to anyone of authority. The story got out (from those who assaulted me), and everyone assumed that I wanted it. When I tried to tell my story, they said I was lying."

"I was afraid I wouldn't get to share my truth. And I did get it, but since it happened with a family member, it was practically swept under the rug."

If you've had any other experiences with domestic violence and/or sexual assault that don't correlate with the questions asked above, please share!

"On more than two occasions, I've been raped by multiple people because of peer pressure to drink/smoke. Once I became intoxicated to the point where I couldn't stand was when they took advantage of me. Afterward, I never spoke up about it and still haven't. I kind of blame myself for giving into the pressure of drinking/smoking excessive amounts beforehand."

"In my health class, we watched a documentary about a girl who had been raped. At the end of the film, we had a class discussion. The class clown proceeded to make numerous jokes and inappropriate comments. My teacher, who is usually very strong-minded and progressive, made very minimal effort to stop him and even laughed along at one point. It was beyond disappointing."

"#BelieveSurvivors, the hardest part after an assault is getting people to believe you or truly understand the depth of what happened. Even if they believe you, they still question, 'How much did you drink?' 'What were you wearing?' 'Did you ever flirt with them before?' They never ask how you're doing, how you're healing."

"I wish there were more resources available for people trying to support a loved one that's experiencing domestic violence or sexual assault."

Chapter

13

Sexually Transmitted Infections

What was your experience like getting tested for STIs?

"Luckily my first and only test has been at a reproductive health center full of comforting staff who really explain and elaborate on any questions or concerns you have, whether you have voiced them or not."

"Very pleasant for the most part. I've always had access to testing through PP and have gotten tested for all possible STIs every time I've gone for reproductive healthcare."

"Finding out my STI status was extremely scary. I didn't really know what to do initially and had no one to talk about it with especially considering the stigma surrounding not only gay men but STIs in general."

"The one time that I thought I had an STI, I was able to get an appointment within a few days, was treated with respect, compassion, and tested negative. I found out very quickly, and it was mostly affordable."

"Accessing PrEP was extremely difficult for me as a minor. Unfortunately, state laws do not support the sale of PrEP to minors without parental consent. Unfortunately, to many teens that are living in households with parents who don't accept them, parental consent is not an option. This is sadly the story for so many young LGBTQ+ identifiers, sadly making PrEP not an option for those at risk."

I started the preface of this book at the age of seventeen, a high schooler, in my Providence, Rhode Island, reproductive health educator cubicle. I am now twenty-one years old sitting in the window seat of my New York City waitressing day job and am a certified prenatal yoga instructor. I would like to say that it is funny how much has changed, though I had hoped to complete this book by the end of my senior year. In March of 2020, the COVID-19 pandemic hit, and our world changed. Four years later, the book was done.

The more I get down on myself for not finishing this book sooner, I think about how throughout the pandemic, the ways of reproductive healthcare have changed immensely—birth work, HIV care, activism, remote sexual health education, the utilization of social media, and so on. There is always more to add, always more storytelling.

If you have made it through to the end of this book, thank you for taking the time to experience shared perspectives and processing these stories. Oftentimes while interviewing, writing, and editing, I had to debrief. They are not easy reads, nor are these topics.

Thank you for your commitment to activism, art, and storytelling. I love you. Let us continue to break the stigma and have these conversations. We won't be silenced!

About the Author

Audrey Lee O'Donnell is a twenty-two-year-old activist, writer, educator, and actress born in Providence, Rhode Island, and now residing in New York City. She began her work in reproductive health and activism at the age of fourteen years old when she initially worked at a Diversity, Equity, and Inclusion Center whilst having volunteered at a coalition against gun violence.

Audrey developed a case study with other High School students at the age of fourteen regarding student rights to walk out during statewide protests, which was then picked up by an Ivy League University.

Audrey streamlined HIV prevention work, co-chaired coalitions on public health events, and connected with a national reproductive health center, where she then worked for three years.

Audrey organized protests advocating for safe, legal abortion with the youth organization she co-founded, taught youth their voting rights and voting registration steps, and assisted with a conference on youth sexual health education, where she was awarded the HIV/STI Community Youth Hero Award.

As Audrey's senior year project in 2019, she interviewed hundreds of people nationally via FaceTime, Google Forms, and in person regarding their experiences on abortion access. During COVID-19 in 2020, the We Won't Be Silenced campaign turned global, and Audrey gained submissions worldwide surrounding topics outside of abortion. As a result, she gained more press, and the *We Won't Be Silenced* book was created.

Audrey hopes to utilize her acting platform in a way that supports her community advocacy work, ensuring that we won't be silenced.

www.ingramcontent.com/pod-product-compliance
Lightning Source LLC
Chambersburg PA
CBHW031652040426
42453CB00006B/277